Spotlight on ANCIENT CIVILIZATIONS
EGYPT

Ancient Egyptian GOVERNMENT

Leigh Rockwood

I0808874

Published in 2014 by The Rosen Publishing Group, Inc.
29 East 21st Street, New York, NY 10010

Copyright © 2014 by The Rosen Publishing Group, Inc.

All rights reserved. No part of this book may be reproduced in any form without permission in writing from the publisher, except by a reviewer.

First Edition

Editor: Jennifer Way
Book Design: Kate Vlachos
Layout Design: Colleen Bialecki

Photo Credits: Cover, pp. 6, 7 (right), 18 DEA/G. Dagli/Orti/De Agostini Picture Library/Getty Images; p. 4 DEA/A. Jemolo/De Agostini Picture Library/Getty Images; p. 5 pavalena/Shutterstock.com; p. 7 (left) Yu Lan/Shutterstock.com; p. 8 DEA/S.Vannini/De Agostini/Getty Images; p. 9 Vladimir Wrangel/Shutterstock.com; pp. 10, 11, 17 Leemage/Universal Images Group/Getty Images; p. 13 GTA Production/Shutterstock.com; p. 14 Kenneth Garrett/National Geographic/Getty Images; p. 15 BasPhoto/Shutterstock.com; p. 19 Universal Images Group/Getty Images; p. 21 Lim Tiaw Leong/Shutterstock.com; p. 23 Stephen Studd/Photographer's Choice/Getty Images.

Library of Congress Cataloging-in-Publication Data

Rockwood, Leigh.
Ancient Egyptian government / by Leigh Rockwood. — 1st ed.
p. cm. — (Spotlight on ancient civilizations. Egypt)
Includes index.
ISBN 978-1-4777-0764-7 (library binding) — ISBN 978-1-4777-0861-3 (pbk.) —
ISBN 978-1-4777-0862-0 (6-pack)
1. Egypt—Politics and government—To 332 B.C.—Juvenile literature. 2. Egypt—Kings and rulers—Juvenile literature. I. Title. II. Series: Spotlight on ancient civilizations. Egypt.
DT61.R5365 2014
932.01—dc23

2012049054

Manufactured in the United States of America

CPSIA Compliance Information: Batch #S13PK2: For Further Information contact Rosen Publishing, New York, New York at 1-800-237-9932

CONTENTS

Ancient Egypt's Beginnings

Ancient Egypt's government changed a lot over its long history. Before 3400 BC, Egypt was made up of many separate kingdoms. Between 3400 BC and 3100 BC, Egypt was a land of two kingdoms, called Upper Egypt and Lower Egypt. The two kingdoms were united in 3100 BC and lasted until 322 BC. This was the ancient Egyptian **civilization** as we think of it today.

Thutmose III, shown here, was pharaoh from 1479 until 1425 BC. His reign was during the Eighteenth Dynasty.

This is a map of modern Egypt. On it you can see the Nile River. It flows northward from Lake Nasser in Upper Egypt to the Mediterranean Sea in Lower Egypt.

When historians talk about ancient Egypt's government, they talk about **dynasties**. A dynasty is a ruling family. A dynasty changed when someone from a different family took over from the current **pharaoh**, or king. There were 31 such dynasties in ancient Egypt.

The Pharaoh

The first pharaoh of ancient Egypt was Narmer, who was also known as Menes. He set up Egypt's capital in the city of Memphis. This was the first national government in the history of the world!

Ancient Egyptians believed that the pharaoh was the god Horus in human form. Because of this belief, ancient Egyptians thought the pharaoh could control things like the Sun and the Nile River.

This is the Narmer Palette. It dates from around 3100 BC, during the First Dynasty. Historians believe it shows Narmer unifying Upper and Lower Egypt.

Left: The god Horus was identified with ancient Egypt's pharaohs. He is sometimes shown as a falcon, like the statue shown here.
Below: This is the pharaoh Tutankhamen's death mask. It is made of gold, with turquoise and other gemstones.

The pharaoh was in charge of all parts of the government. He controlled trade, the military, and the temples. The pharaoh also owned most of the land in his kingdom.

The Great Royal Wife

While most ancient Egyptian men had only one wife, pharaohs had several wives at once. This allowed the pharaoh to marry the daughters of **allies** to strengthen political relationships. The Great Royal Wife was a special title for the pharaoh's main wife, which set her apart in status from the other wives.

This statue of Hatshepsut shows her wearing a false beard, which was a symbol of the pharaoh's power.

Nefertiti was the Great Royal Wife of Akhenaten, a pharaoh during the Eighteenth Dynasty.

Hatshepsut was the Great Royal Wife to Thutmose II. After his death, she crowned herself **regent**. She later ruled as pharaoh and ruled longer than any other woman in ancient Egypt. She did this because her stepson Thutmose III was next in line for the throne but was still a baby.

The Vizier

The **vizier** was the highest-ranking official serving the pharaoh. He was chosen by the pharaoh for this role and reported directly to him. The vizier's duty was to supervise the day-to-day running of the country. He was in charge of all government officials and their departments. He also sat on the High Court.

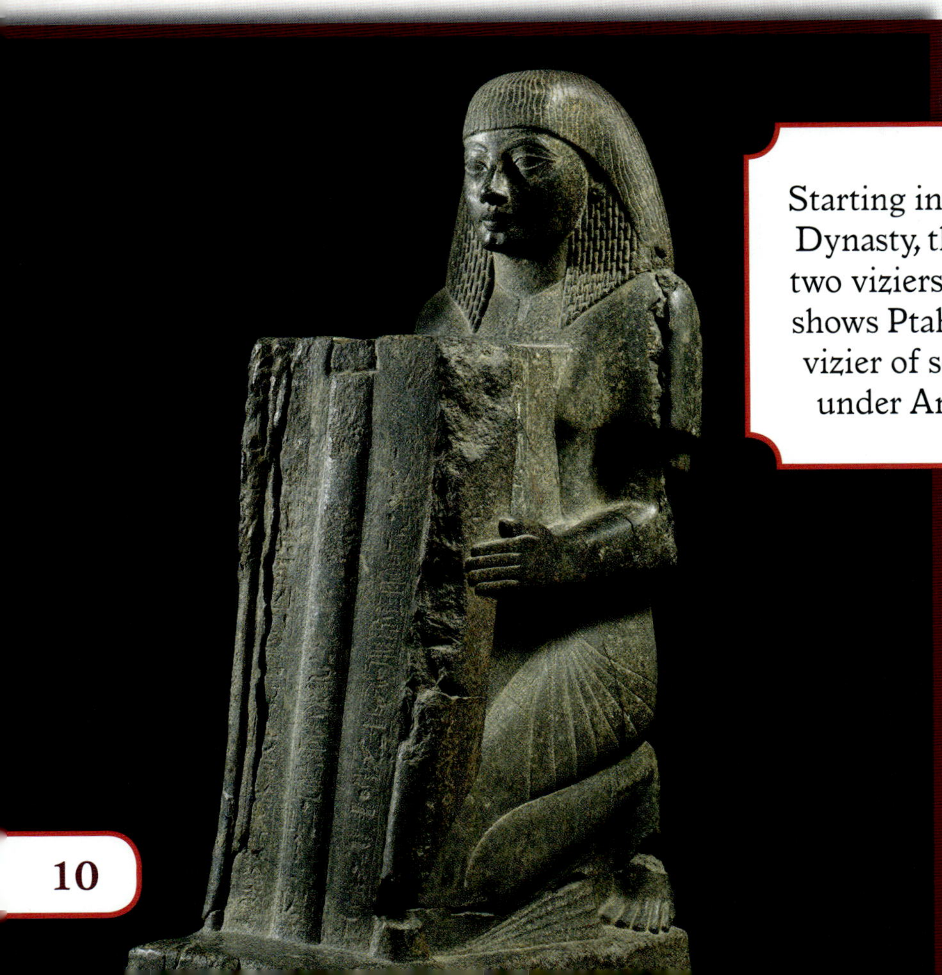

Starting in the Eighteenth Dynasty, there were often two viziers. This sculpture shows Ptahmose, who was vizier of southern Egypt under Amenhotep III.

This painting shows people counting and recording a wheat harvest so that the grain could be taxed. Viziers were in charge of making sure that taxes were collected.

In a document describing the code of behavior of the vizier, there were three main things expected of him. He was expected to act according to the law. He was expected to make fair judgments. Finally, he was expected to uphold Egypt's laws.

The Division of Power

In ancient Egypt, the pharaoh ruled over everyone else. Below the pharaoh was a **hierarchy** of officials. First among these were the vizier and the high priests. The vizier was the pharaoh's highest-ranking government official. The high priests were the pharaoh's highest-ranking priests for the kingdom's gods. Judges, **scribes**, nobles, and other priests filled important roles below the vizier and the high priests.

Below these important officials were other officials, who were in charge of people such as craftsmen, farmers, and soldiers. It is important to remember that everyone ultimately obeyed the orders of the pharaoh, who sat at the top of the hierarchy.

Scribes wrote up official government records. They wrote using hieroglyphics like the ones shown on this picture.

Maat in Ancient Egypt

Little survives of ancient Egyptian laws. However, we do know that ancient Egyptians' system of laws was based on the ideal of Maat. This was the concept of justice and balance. The pharaoh and the government were responsible for making laws that upheld the ideal of Maat.

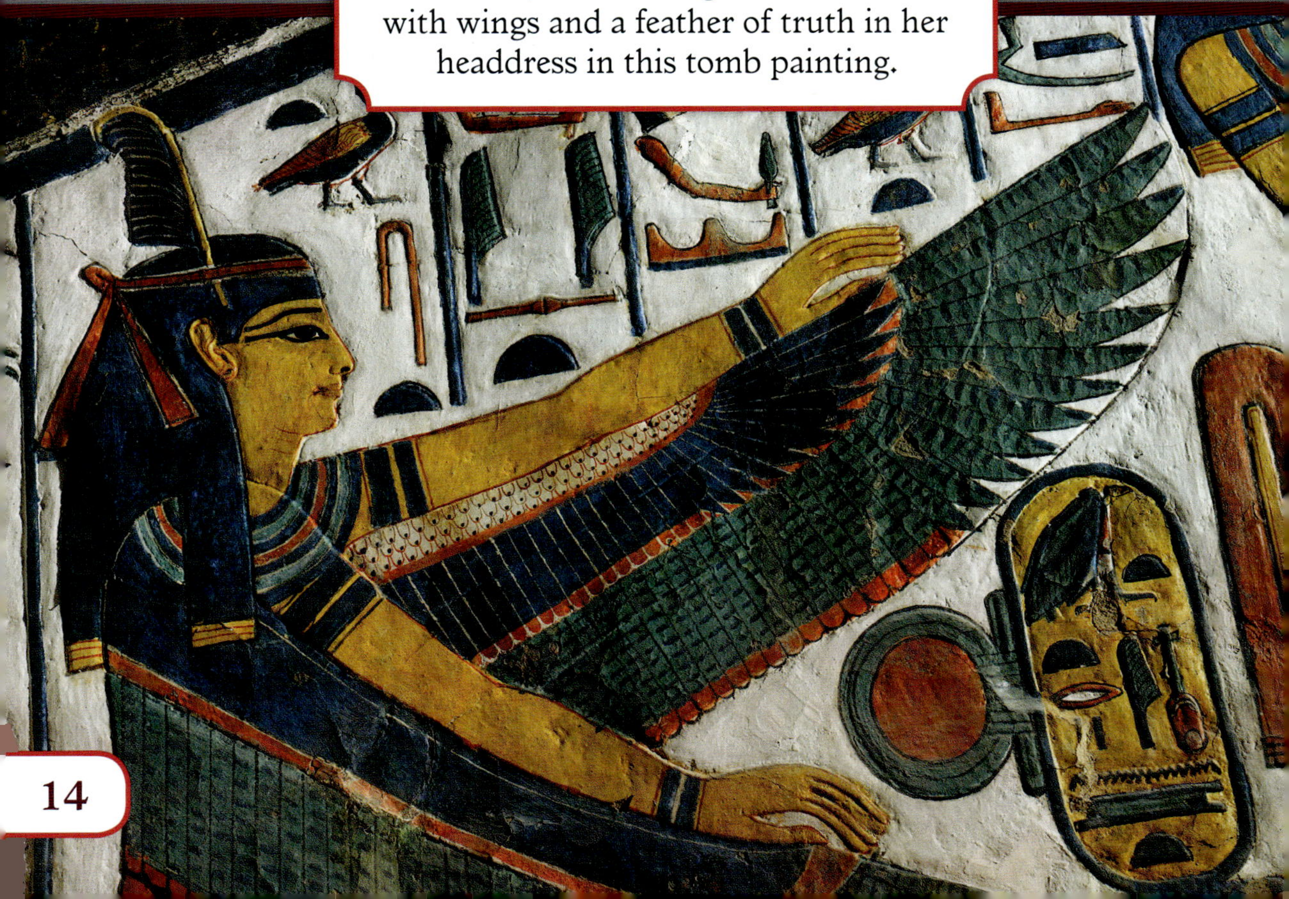

Maat was also the name of the goddess of truth and justice. The goddess is shown with wings and a feather of truth in her headdress in this tomb painting.

This stone carving shows the pharaoh Ramses II enslaving people he defeated in battle. Slaves had fewer rights than other people in ancient Egypt.

Women and men were seen as having different roles in life but were treated nearly equally under ancient Egyptian law. Women could work, own property, and divorce. Although there was a big difference in social standing between people from the upper classes and the lower classes, the ideal of Maat valued fairness in how laws were applied to ancient Egyptians.

Crime and Courts

There were two main courts in ancient Egypt. The Kenbet was the local court. It handled minor claims and disputes between people. The Great Kenbet was the High Court, located in the capital. The vizier oversaw it. This court handled large land purchases and serious crimes.

When people broke the law in ancient Egypt, they were tried and punished through the courts. Minor crimes might be punished by fines or beatings. More serious crimes were punished by disfigurement, such as having a nose or ear cut off. Death was the punishment for the worst crimes, such as murder or robbing tombs.

Scribes made documents of court trials, so that they could be saved for future reference. This one records the trial of tomb robbers.

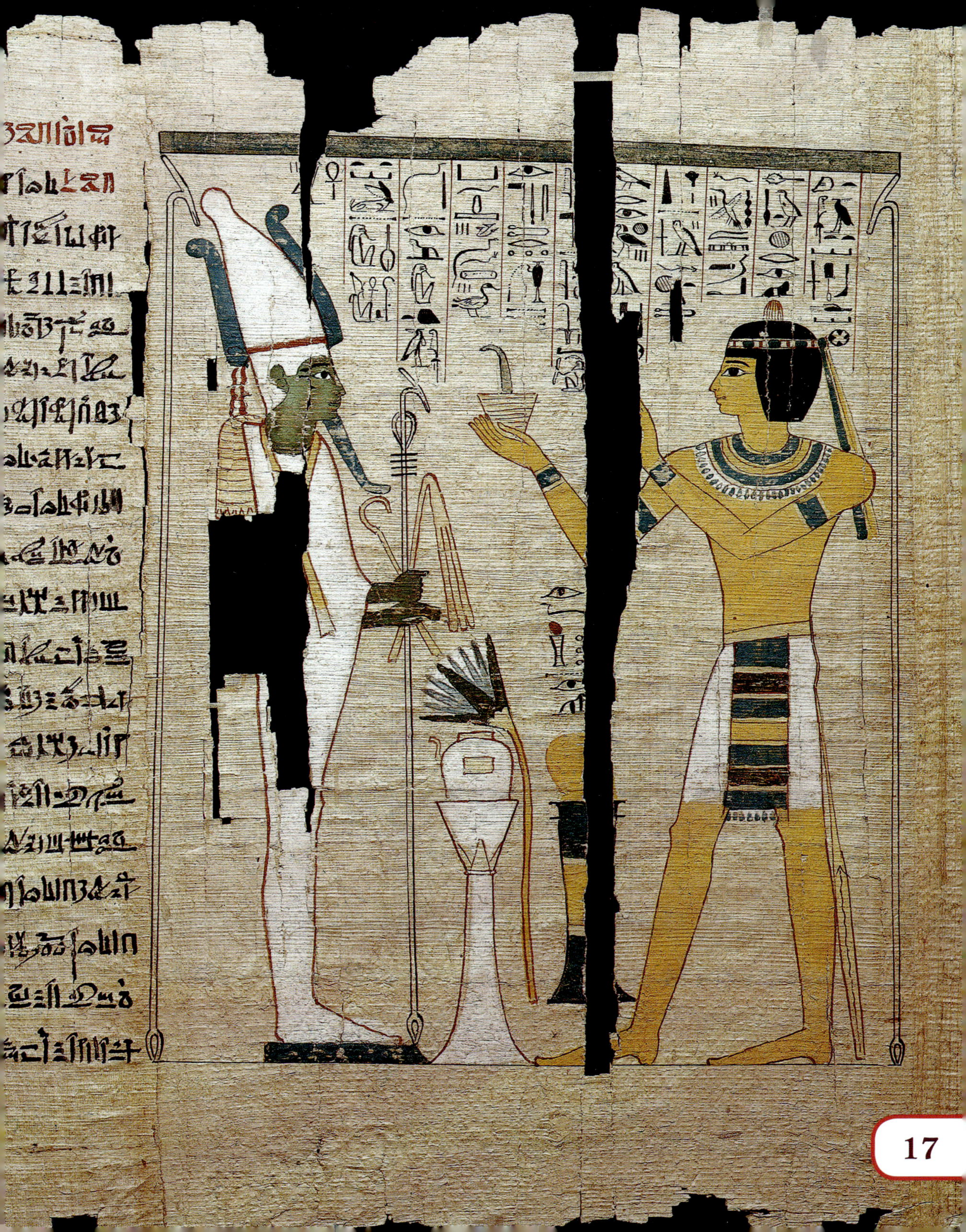

The Army

The first ancient Egyptian pharaohs had only a basic army armed with spears and shields. Temple and tomb paintings show pharaohs leading their armies into battle. Around 1700 BC, the Hyksos, who lived across the Sinai Peninsula, took control of Egypt. They brought with them better weapons, such as the **composite bow** and **chariots**. The Egyptians made improvements to these weapons, which helped them defeat the Hyksos and regain control around 1560 BC.

At times, ancient Egypt paid foreigners to fight with its army. These wooden models show a group of Nubian soldiers fighting for Egypt. Nubia was a kingdom to Egypt's south.

This temple carving shows the pharaoh Ramses II leading his army into battle.

After the Egyptians defeated the Hyksos, they had a more powerful army. They were able to defend their country from foreign invaders. They were also able to expand their empire by conquering other lands.

The Navy

Ancient Egypt had one of the world's earliest navies. The main role of the navy was to carry soldiers, supplies, and communication to other parts of the empire.

The ancient Egyptian navy also fought battles, though. One of the most famous was the Battle Against the Sea Peoples, which happened during the reign of Ramses III. The Sea Peoples were conquering lands along the Mediterranean Sea. The pharaoh used his navy's fast, **maneuverable** ships to trap the Sea Peoples' bulkier and slower ships. The Egyptians defeated the Sea Peoples in this battle and kept them from invading their empire.

Ports have existed along Egypt's Mediterranean coast since ancient times. The port in this photograph is near today's Alexandria.

A Rigid System

In ancient Egypt, most government positions were **hereditary**. That means that roles such as pharaoh, vizier, or priest were passed from father to son. People also generally married within their own class. This meant that there was not much of a chance for people in the lower classes to move up in the world.

Such a rigid system is not fair by modern standards. However, the hereditary system is partly what gave ancient Egypt's government stability. The stability of Egypt's government enabled the civilization to last for nearly 3,000 years.

This statue of the pharaoh Ramses II stands at the entrance of a temple in Luxor, Egypt. Such tombs and temples were built for only the highest-ranking people, such as pharaohs, Great Royal Wives, viziers, and nobles.

GLOSSARY

allies (A-lyz) Countries that are friendly and that help each other in times of crisis.

chariots (CHAR-ee-uts) Two-wheeled battle cars pulled by horses.

civilization (sih-vih-lih-ZAY-shun) People living in a certain way.

composite bow (kom-PO-zut BOH) A bow made of horn, wood, and animal tissue.

dynasties (DY-nas-teez) Lines of rulers who belong to the same families.

hereditary (huh-REH-dih-teh-ree) Passed down by an ancestor from generation to generation.

hierarchy (HY-eh-rar-kee) A ruling body arranged by rank or class.

maneuverable (muh-NOO-veh-ruh-bel) Can get into or out of a position easily.

pharaoh (FER-oh) An ancient Egyptian ruler.

regent (REE-jent) A person who governs in place of a royal who is unable to rule.

scribes (SKRYBZ) People whose job is to copy books by hand.

vizier (vuh-ZIR) The highest-ranking official serving the pharaoh.

INDEX

WEBSITES

Due to the changing nature of Internet links, PowerKids Press has developed an online list of websites related to the subject of this book. This site is updated regularly. Please use this link to access the list: www.powerkidslinks.com/sace/gov/